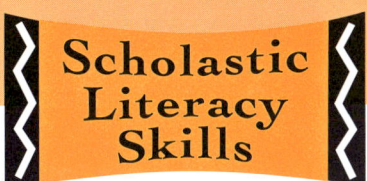

Comprehension
Key Stage 2

Pupil's book

Editor	Kate Pearce
Series designer	Joy White
Designer	Heather C Sanneh
Cover illustration	Joy White
Illustrations	David B. Jones

Designed using Adobe Pagemaker
Processed by Scholastic Ltd, Leamington Spa

Published by Scholastic Ltd, Villiers House, Clarendon Avenue, Leamington Spa, Warwickshire CV32 5PR

Text © 1998 Claire Colling
© 1998 Scholastic Ltd

234567890   8901234567

British Library Cataloguing-in-Publication Data
A catalogue record for this book is available from the British Library.

ISBN 0-590-53888-8

All rights reserved. This book is sold subject to the condition that it shall not, by way of trade or otherwise, be lent, hired out or otherwise circulated without the publisher's prior consent in any form of binding or cover other than that in which it is published and without a similar condition, including this condition, being imposed upon the subsequent purchaser.

No part of this publication may be reproduced, stored in a retrieval system, or transmitted, in any form or by any means, electronic, mechanical, photocopying, recording or otherwise, without the prior permission of the publisher.

Contents

Unit 1	Recount	
Abed's special day		4

Unit 2	Instruction	
How to wash your hands		6

Unit 3	Drama	
Trouble in the park		8

Unit 4	Narrative	
The new girl		10

Unit 5	Report	
Whales		12

Unit 6	Recount	
Our school trip to the farm		14

Unit 7	Explanation	
Why do we need fire?		16

Unit 8	Argument	
More care should be taken with rubbish		18

Unit 9	Instruction	
How to cross the road safely		20

Unit 10	Poetry	
Sounds		22

Unit 11	Drama	
The boy who cried 'Wolf'		24

Unit 12	Narrative	
The little dog and the big, juicy bone		26

Unit 13	Report	
Planet Earth		28

Unit 14	Narrative	
The naughty kittens		30

Unit 15	Explanation	
Why is the Sun important?		32

Unit 16	Argument	
You should look after your teeth		34

Unit 17	Poetry	
In our playground		36

Unit 18	Narrative	
Sally Ann – Princess of the Chip Kingdom		38

Unit 19	Instruction	
How to make cheese on toast		40

Unit 20	Explanation	
Why do some animals sleep in winter?		42

Unit 21	Argument	
Being able to swim can save your life		44

Unit 22	Argument	
Exercise is good for you!		46

Unit 23	Poetry	
Time flies		48

Unit 24	Narrative	
The strange plant		50

Unit 25	Narrative	
The magic pencil		52

Unit 26	Poetry	
On the beach		54

Unit 27	Drama	
In the rainforest		56

Unit 28	Narrative	
A trip to the future		58

Unit 29	Explanation	
How a guitar makes a sound		60

Unit 30	Report	
Dinosaurs		62

Recount

Abed's special day

This is a **recount** of Abed's special day. A **recount** tells you about **something that happened in the past**.

Before you read

✿ Can you remember a day that has been special to you?
✿ Why was this day special?

Read this story.

ABED'S SPECIAL DAY

On Friday I went to the seaside. The sun was very hot. It was a special day for me because I had never seen the sea before.

When I saw the blue sea, I felt very happy. On the beach I took off my sandals and ran along the soft sand.

I got out my bucket and spade and made the best sandcastle anyone had ever seen. It had ten big towers and I made a moat around the sandcastle with sea water. Everyone stopped to look at my sandcastle. That made me feel very pleased and proud.

As we got in the car to go home I felt sad. The sea had got closer and closer to my sandcastle.

I wonder if my sandcastle is still there today?

Re-read the story and answer the following questions.

1 Where did Abed go on Friday?

2 How did Abed feel when he saw the blue sea?

3 What did Abed do before he ran along the sand?

4 Why do you think people stopped to look at Abed's sandcastle?

5 What do you think people were wearing on the beach? Why?

6 What do you think people were doing on the beach?

7 Why was this day so special for Abed?

8 Why was Abed sad at the end of the story?

9 Do you think Abed's sandcastle is still there today? Why?

10 A recount uses words in the past tense. For example:

Present tense   **Past tense**
run   ran

Now put these words in the past tense. (Use the story to help you.)
take
make
feel

More things to do

Write about a day which has been special to you. Remember to say how you *felt* on that day and *why* the day was special to you.

Unit 2

How to wash your hands

An **instruction** tells you how to do something.

Before you read

❋ Why do you need to wash your hands?
❋ When should you wash your hands?

Read these instructions.

How to wash your hands

You will need
a sink
soap
water

Instructions
1 Fill the sink with warm water.
2 Wet your hands.
3 Put some soap on your hands.
4 Rub the soap all over your hands.
5 Rinse your hands in the water.
6 Empty the sink.
7 Dry your hands.

Re-read the instructions and answer the following questions.

1 Write this sentence in your notebook and then complete it.
   These instructions tell you how to _____ _____ _____ .

2 Name two things you need to wash your hands.

3 Write out these instructions in your notebook in the correct order.
   Rinse your hands in the water.
   Put some soap on your hands.
   Wet your hands.

4 Would you use cold or warm water to wash your hands? Why?

5 When did you wash your hands today?

6 You can use a sink to wash your hands. Where can you wash your whole body?

7 Every sentence in these instructions begins with a verb (a doing word), for example 'Fill' and 'Wet'. Pick out two other verbs.

8 What would you use to dry your hands?

9 We need to wash our bodies, but can you think of any other things that we need to wash around the house?

10 Why are there numbers before the instructions?

More things to do

Write down the things you would need and a set of instructions for 'How to wash your hair'.

Drama

Trouble in the park

In a **play** people act out a story by learning words from a **script** and saying them to each other.

Before you read

❀ Look at the title of this play. What do you think it might be about?
❀ Have you ever lost something important? How did you feel about losing it?

Now read the play.

TROUBLE IN THE PARK

Chloe is talking to her brother Tim. They are playing in the park. Chloe wants to go home because it is getting late.

CHLOE: Come on, Tim, let's go home. It's getting late.
TIM: I'm not going home until I find my watch. It must be here somewhere.
CHLOE: Are you sure you didn't leave it at home?
TIM: No, because I remember taking it off to play football. I put it in my pocket.
CHLOE: Well, I've looked in those bushes.
TIM: And I've looked on the grass.
CHLOE: You'll have to go home without it. Don't cry, Tim. It will turn up.
TIM: I can't go home without it. It was a present from Aunty Jenny. I'll get told off if I go home without it.
CHLOE: You'll get told off anyway if you don't go home soon. It's past six o'clock! If I get told off as well, it will be your fault!
TIM: Oh no! Here comes mum, and she doesn't look very happy!

Re-read the play with a friend, then answer the following questions.

1 Where does the play take place?

2 What has Tim lost?

3 Where does Tim remember putting his watch?

4 What do you think could have happened to his watch?

5 Why was Tim worried about going home?

6 Why do you think the children have to be home before six o'clock?

7 Why do you think Tim and Chloe's mum did not look very happy?

8 How do we know that Tim is unhappy?

9 How do you think Tim and Chloe felt when they saw their mum? Why?

10 Write down what you think their mum will say.

More things to do

When people speak in a play, we call this dialogue. Chloe and Tim will have to explain to their mum what has happened. Can you write down the dialogue they will use (the things they will say).

Narrative

Unit 4

The new girl

A story has one or more characters. **Characters** are the main people in a story.

Before you read

❖ Have you got a special friend?
❖ Have you ever fallen out with your friend?

Read this story.

THE NEW GIRL

Rebecca and Kerry were best friends. They sat next to each other in class. Rebecca and Kerry were both tall, with long dark hair. Everyone thought they were sisters.

One day, Rebecca couldn't go to school because she had a bad cold. So Kerry had to sit on her own in class, but not for long.

'Good morning, everybody. Today we have a new pupil. Her name is Sarah,' said the teacher, Mr Blake. 'Sit next to Kerry, Sarah. Kerry can tell you all about your new school.'

Kerry and Sarah soon made friends. They were both very good at dancing and Mr Blake asked them to make up a dance for the school show.

After a few days, Rebecca was better and came back to school.

'So what are we going to do for the school show, Kerry?' asked Rebecca.

Kerry went very red. 'Well, I'm dancing with Sarah,' said Kerry.

Rebecca walked off and gave Sarah a nasty look. Rebecca and Kerry didn't talk to each other all morning.

Later that day Kerry found Rebecca talking to Sarah in the playground. They were both smiling.

'Sarah's had a great idea,' said Rebecca. 'She's asked Mr Blake if the three of us can make up a dance for the school show.'

'So are we friends again?' asked Kerry hopefully.

'You bet!' said Rebecca smiling.

Re-read the story and answer the following questions.

1 Who are the main characters in this story?

2 What did Rebecca and Kerry look like?

3 Why did everyone think that Rebecca and Kerry were sisters?

4 What was the name of the teacher?

5 What was the name of the new girl?

6 Why couldn't Rebecca go to school?

7 How do you think Sarah felt on her first day in a new school?

8 Why was Rebecca upset when she came back to school?

9 What was Sarah's great idea?

10 Is the ending a happy ending? Why?

More things to do

Write down what you think makes a good friend. Use these words to help you:

| cares | funny | play | shares |
| kind | trust | talk | helps |

Narrative

Unit 5 — Report

Whales

Reports tell you **true information** (facts) about something. All these are facts:
- Whales live in seas and oceans.
- Whales are very big.
- Whales can swim well.

Before you read

❉ Can you think of any other animals which live in the sea?
❉ Could we live in the sea?

Read this report.

WHALES

Whales live in seas and oceans, but they need air to breathe. Whales can hold their breath for an hour or more under water, but then they come up to the top of the sea to breathe. They have flippers to help them swim. Most whales eat sea plants called plankton. You cannot see plankton because they are very small.

The blue whale is the largest animal in the world. It can be 30 metres long. That is about as long as two buses. It can weigh as much as 100 tons. That is about the weight of 20 elephants!

Whales can talk to each other by making noises under water. Some whales can communicate with each other even when they are over 100 kilometres apart!

Some whales are hunted and killed, but most countries in the world now try to protect whales.

Re-read the report and answer the following questions.

1 Where do whales live?

2 For how long can whales hold their breath?

3 Which is the largest animal in the world?

4 What do most whales eat?

5 What do whales have to help them to swim?

6 Whales use their flippers to swim around. Can you think of two ways we use our legs to move around?

7 Which fact tells you that the blue whale is heavy?

8 Why do you think we should protect whales?

9 This report contains many facts, such as 'Whales live in seas and oceans'. Can you pick out two other facts about whales?

More things to do

Using an information book, or the computer, find out some facts about a different sea animal and write a short report about it. Remember to include these facts in your work: how it moves, where it lives, how big it is, what it eats.

Recount

Our school trip to the farm

This is a **recount** about what happened when Class 3C went on a school trip to the farm. A recount tells you about **something that happened in the past**.

Before you read

- Write down the animals which you think might live on a farm.
- What do you think a farmer might grow on his farm?

Read this recount.

OUR SCHOOL TRIP TO THE FARM

Last week everyone in Class 3C went on a school trip to a farm. Farmer Jones showed us around the farm. We all had to wear wellington boots. Steven, of course, kept trying to splash everyone with mud.

Farmer Jones told us about the crops he grew in the fields, such as wheat, barley and corn. He also took us to see lots of animals. There were big black and white cows, beautiful horses in the field and pigs playing in the mud.

Everyone liked the hens best. They kept trying to peck our clothes. Steven tried to give one a chocolate bar, but the farmer said hens didn't eat chocolate.

When we were walking back to the coach we heard a yell. Steven had fallen over. He was covered from head to toe in mud. Everyone (apart from Steven) thought that was the best part of the trip!

Re-read the recount and answer the following questions.

1 What was the farmer called?

2 Why do you think the children had to wear wellington boots?

3 Who was always naughty?

4 Which animals did the children see at the farm?

5 Which animals were in the field?

6 Can you think of something you eat that is made from wheat?

7 How do you think the children felt when Steven kept splashing them with mud?

8 Why did the children think the best part of the trip was when Steven fell in the mud?

9 Name some other animals you might find on a farm.

10 In the story there are lots of nouns. Nouns are names of things, such as 'horse', 'crops', 'clothes'. Use the story to help you find the missing nouns to add to these sentences. Write the answers in your notebook.

Last week everyone in Class 3C went on a school trip to a _____.
Steven kept trying to splash everyone with _____.
There were big black and white _____.
The hens in the yard kept coming up and trying to peck the children's _____.
The children were walking back to the _____ when they heard a yell.

Now pick out some other nouns from the story.

More things to do

Find out more about farm animals. Choose one farm animal to draw and write about. Think about the sound it makes, what it looks like and what it eats.

Explanation

Why do we need fire?

An **explanation** can tell you why something is important.

Before you read

✿ What makes your house warm?
✿ How can fire help people? How can fire be dangerous?

Read this explanation.

WHY DO WE NEED FIRE?

Fire is a hot flame. You can make fire by burning something, but you must take care because fire can be dangerous. Fire needs air and fuel to make a flame. Fuel includes things such as wood, coal, gas or oil.

We need fire because it gives off heat and light. Fire is useful because we can use it to cook food. It can also heat houses to keep them warm. Fire can also be used to melt metal in factories. The metal can then be used to make things such as cars.

Many years ago, people used fire to see in the dark. They lit their rooms with the flames from candles and oil lamps.

Fire can be useful, but it can also be harmful. If a fire is spreading and becoming dangerous we need trained firefighters to put it out.

Re-read the explanation and answer the following questions.

1 What is fire?

2 What does fire need to make a flame?

3 What does fire give off which can make you cough?

4 In the past, people used the flames from candles to light rooms. What do most people use today to light rooms?

5 Why do we need firefighters?

6 The writer says fire can be useful and harmful. Look up the words 'useful' and 'harmful' in your dictionary, then think about the two questions below. Write some answers in your notebook.
How can fire be useful?
How can fire be harmful?

7 Which number would you dial if you spotted a fire?

8 Write these sentences in your notebook, marking each one true or false.
Fire needs air to burn.
Fire can melt metal.
We cannot use fire to heat food.

9 These sentences are in the wrong order. In your notebooks, write them in the same order as they appear in the explanation.
If a fire is spreading and becoming dangerous we need trained firefighters to put it out.
Many years ago, people used fire to see in the dark.
Fire is a hot flame.

More things to do

Think of some adjectives (describing words) to describe the flames of a fire. Think about the colour of the flames, the noise they make and their shape.

Write a short explanation that tells people about Bonfire Night. Write about when it happens, why it happens and what you can see on Bonfire Night.

Argument

More care should be taken with rubbish

An **argument** tells you someone's **point of view**.

Before you read

❂ Think of two things you have thrown away this week.
❂ What happens to rubbish when you throw it away?

Now read this argument.

More care should be taken with rubbish

Rubbish is something we throw away because we do not want it. Rubbish can include old tins and cans, glass and plastic bottles, crisp packets, old newspapers, and lots more...

When we throw rubbish away, we should make sure it goes into a dustbin. Some people, though, throw their rubbish on the ground. This can make a place look dirty and messy.

Rubbish in dustbins is taken away to rubbish tips. Some is burned and some is buried. Some rubbish can be harmful. People can cut themselves on broken glass and tins. Rubbish can also be dangerous to animals and birds. They might eat the rubbish by mistake or they might get stuck inside the empty bottles or tins.

Some rubbish, instead of being disposed of, can be used again. This is called recycling. Items that can be recycled include newspapers and bottles. People should sort their rubbish into things that can be recycled and then take these items to the recycling containers.

People should take more care with their rubbish so that places are kept clean and safe.

Re-read the argument and answer the following questions.

1 Name three things which people throw away.

2 Why do some people throw their rubbish on the ground?

3 Where is rubbish in dustbins taken?

4 Why can rubbish be dangerous to animals and birds?

5 Which animals might look for food in empty cans or bottles?

6 Why do you think rubbish tips can be dangerous places for children to play?

7 Which would be better, burying or burning rubbish? Would there be other better ways?

8 How does the writer want us to take care with our rubbish?

9 In your notebook, fill in the missing words in these sentences. Use the argument to help you.
Rubbish is something we _____ away because we do not want it.
People can _____ themselves on broken glass and tins.
When rubbish is used again, it is called _____ .

More things to do

Design a poster which asks people not to drop their litter on the floor.

Unit 9

Instruction

How to cross the road safely

Instructions tell you how to do something.

Before you read

✿ Why can it be dangerous crossing the road?
✿ What is the Green Cross Code?

Read these instructions.

HOW TO CROSS THE ROAD SAFELY

1. Find a safe place to cross (a pedestrian crossing).
2. Stand near the kerb.
3. Press the crossing button and wait.
4. Wait for the traffic lights to turn red to stop the traffic.
5. Wait for the 'walking person' to turn from red to green.
6. Look right, look left, look right again and if all is safe walk quickly across the road.
7. Keep looking and listening as you cross.

Answer the following questions.

1. What do the instructions tell you?

2. How many instructions are there?

3. Write these instructions in your notebook in the correct order.
   Wait for the 'walking person' to turn from red to green.
   Press the crossing button and wait.
   Find a safe place to cross (a pedestrian crossing).

4. Why is it important to look and listen when you are crossing the road?

5. Who helps *you* to cross roads?

6. What other things can help us to cross the road safely?

7 Cars use the road. What other things use the road?

8 Do you think these are important instructions? Why?

More things to do

In your notebook, fill in the missing words for these instructions. Use these words to help you.

safe   looking   traffic   listen   place
near   listening   straight   cars

Find a _____ _____ to cross, away from parked _____.
Stop _____ the kerb.
Look all around and _____.
Let the _____ pass.
If there is no traffic near, walk _____ across the road.
As you cross the road, keep _____ and _____.

Design a poster for your school which explains to pupils the correct way to cross a road.

Poetry

Sounds

In this **poem**, the poet uses her sense of hearing to tell us about the sounds she loves and the sounds she hates.

Before you read

- Close your eyes. What sounds can you hear?
- What are your favourite sounds?
- What sounds do you hate?

Read this poem.

SOUNDS

I love the sound of cats purring,
I hate the sound of glass breaking,
I love the sound of music playing,
I hate the sound of paper tearing,
I love the sound of birds singing,
I hate the sound of whistles blowing,
I love the sound of water gushing,
I hate the sound of dogs barking,
I love the sound of trees rustling,
I hate the sound of thunder crashing,
I love the sound of crisps crunching,
I hate the sound of bees buzzing.

Claire Colling

Re-read the poem with a friend. Take it in turns to read a line each. Now answer these questions.

1 Which animal does the poet like to hear purring?

2 Which sound does water make in the poem?

3 Can you think of any other sounds that water makes?

4 Which animals make a barking sound?

5 Why do you think trees make a rustling sound?

6 Which music do *you* like to hear playing?

7 Where might you hear a whistle blowing?

8 Which sound do you like best in this poem? Why?

9 Why do you think the poet hates the sound of thunder?

10 A lot of the words in the poem end in 'ing'. Write these sentences in your notebooks and fill in the gaps with these SOUND words:

banging   whistling   roaring   crackling   squeaking

A fire makes a _____ sound.
A lion makes a _____ sound.
A drum makes a _____ sound.
A mouse makes a _____ sound.
The wind makes a _____ sound.

More things to do

Make up your own sounds poem. Write about sounds you love and sounds you hate. Read your poem to the class. Do other children love and hate the same sounds as you?

Unit 11 — Drama

The boy who cried 'Wolf'

A **play** has characters who speak. When they speak we call this **dialogue**.

Before you read

❁ Have you ever felt bored?
❁ Have you ever played a trick on anyone? What happened?

Here are the characters in the play:

    Boy   First Person   Second Person   Wolf

Read this play.

THE BOY WHO CRIED 'WOLF'

A bored boy sits alone at the top of a hill. He has sheep all around him. The boy sees two people walking along the path at the bottom of the hill.

BOY: Help! Help! A wolf is here! My sheep are in danger.
FIRST PERSON: Where is the wolf?
BOY: Come with me!
(The people follow the boy to the top of the hill.)
SECOND PERSON: Which way did the wolf go?
(The boy laughs.)
BOY: I played a trick on you. There isn't really a wolf.
(The people walk back down the hill.)
BOY: That was funny, I'll try it again. Help! Help! The wolf is here by the tree. He is going to eat my sheep.
FIRST PERSON: There may be a wolf now. We had better go and see.
(They walk up the hill again.)
SECOND PERSON: There is no wolf here. You have played a trick on us again.
(They walk down the hill again.)
BOY: That was great fun. These people thought the wolf was going to eat my sheep.
(The boy laughs and sits by the tree. A wolf comes creeping towards him.)
WOLF: Those sheep look tasty. But you look even tastier!

(The boy jumps up and turns around to see the wolf.)
BOY: Help! Help! The wolf is here!
FIRST PERSON: We're not coming this time. We don't like your silly tricks. We know you're lying and there's no wolf.
BOY: Please come. There really IS a wolf this time!
(The people walk away. The boy keeps calling.)
WOLF: That will teach you to play tricks!

Re-read the play and answer the following questions.

1 How many characters are there in the play?

2 Where is the boy?

3 Why does the boy play a trick on the people?

4 How do you think the people felt when they found out they had been tricked?

5 Who did the wolf want to eat?

6 How do you think the boy felt when he saw the wolf?

7 Why didn't the people believe the boy when there really was a wolf?

8 What lesson do you think the boy learned?

9 In the play there are words in brackets like this: *(The boy laughs.)*
   These are called stage directions: they tell you how to act on stage. Write down two other stage directions you can find in the play.

More things to do

Read the play again and then act it out. Remember: you need to be in a group of four. Decide who is going to play which part. Act out your play to another group or to the rest of the class. Do not forget to follow the stage directions.

Unit 12

Narrative

The little dog and the big, juicy bone

A **fable** is a story which tells you about how people behave. There is sometimes a **message** in the story.

Before you read

❁ Have you ever helped someone to do something?
❁ Do you share things? Which things do you share?

Read this narrative.

THE LITTLE DOG AND THE BIG, JUICY BONE

One day, a little dog was walking through the forest. He was feeling very happy and proud because he had a big, juicy bone. On his way, he met a tiny mouse.

'That's a lovely bone,' said the tiny mouse. 'May I have some?'

'No, you can't!' said the little dog. 'It's my bone and I'm going to eat it all on my own,' and he trotted off. Then he met a rabbit.

'My, that looks a tasty bone,' said the rabbit. 'Could I try some?'

'No, you can't!' said the little dog. 'It's my bone and I'm going to eat it all on my own,' and he carried on along the path.

The little dog said the same thing to the snake and the frog.

After a while, the dog sat down to rest near a lake. He looked down at the water and to his surprise he could see another bone. The bone in the water looked even better than his bone.

'I think I'll have that bone instead,' he said to himself. He opened his mouth to reach for the bone and dropped his bone into the water. He watched it sink to the bottom of the lake. He looked for the bone he had seen in the water – but it had gone!

Now the little dog was left with no bone at all. He called out to the mouse, rabbit, snake and frog. 'Please help me get my bone back,' he begged.

'No, we won't!' they shouted. The little dog sat down and cried. The other animals soon felt sorry for him.

'Don't worry,' said the rabbit and he asked his friend the fish to swim down to the bottom of the lake to fetch the bone.

'Thank you,' said the little dog and they all sat down together to share the big, juicy bone.

Re-read the story and answer the following questions.

1. Why was the little dog happy and proud at the start of the story?

2. Which animal did the little dog meet first?

3. How many animals did the little dog meet altogether?

4. What do you think the dog said to the snake and the frog when they asked him if they could have some of his bone?

5. How did the little dog get the bone back?

6. Was there really another bone? Explain your answer.

7. Why do you think the other animals would not help the little dog get his bone back at first?

8. Does the story have a happy ending? Why?

9. What do you think the message is in this story?

10. In this story, speech marks are used to tell us when someone is speaking. Write these sentences in your notebook and put in the speech marks in the correct places.
    That's a lovely bone, said the tiny mouse.
    Please help me get my bone back, he begged.
    Don't worry, said the rabbit.

More things to do

Can you tell the story using pictures? Here are some ideas. You could draw the dog with his bone. The dog meeting the animals. The dog losing his bone in the lake. The fish getting the bone. All the animals together sharing the bone. When you have drawn the pictures, write what is happening underneath each one.

Unit 13

Report

Planet Earth

A **report** gives us **true information** (facts) about something. This report tells us facts about the planet we call Earth.

Before you read

❀ Do you know the names of any other planets?
❀ What shape is planet Earth?

Read this report.

PLANET EARTH

There are many planets in space. Earth is one of the nine planets in our Solar System. It is the only planet that we know of where there are living things. This is because living things, such as plants and animals, need water to live.

Water covers a lot of the planet called Earth. There are oceans, seas, rivers and lakes. If you could look at Earth from space you would see why astronauts call it 'The blue planet'.

The Earth moves around the Sun. It takes 365 days (one year) to move around the Sun. As the Earth moves, it spins round. Because it spins, we have day and night. When our part of the Earth is turned away from the Sun it is night-time. When our part of the Earth is turned towards the Sun it is daytime.

Re-read the report and answer the following questions.

1 How many planets are there in our Solar System?

2 What do all living things need to live?

3 Why do you think astronauts call Earth 'The blue planet'?

4 What is an astronaut?

5 How long does it take the Earth to move around the Sun?

6 How do we know there are other planets?

7 Complete these sentences.
   The Earth moves around the _____.
   Water covers a lot of the _____.

8 Write these sentences in your notebook, marking each one true or false.
   The Earth is one of ten planets.
   It takes 365 months to move around the Sun.
   As the Earth moves, it spins round.

9 If you were sent off to explore a new planet, what would you take with you in the rocket?

More things to do

Here are some facts about Mars. Write your own report using these facts: Mars is called the Red Planet. It has many red rocks and dust. Mars has many craters. Mars is very cold at night-time and in winter. There are many dust storms on Mars. You would not be able to breathe on Mars.

Narrative

Unit 14

The naughty kittens

A story has three parts: a **beginning**, a **middle** and an **end**.

Before you read

❂ What animals do people keep as pets?
❂ How would you look after a pet?

Read this story.

THE NAUGHTY KITTENS

Beginning
Once there were two little kittens called Tilly and Tommy. Tilly was ginger with little white paws and Tommy was black and white with a black tail. They lived with their owner in a large house.

Middle
One day, their owner had to go out to do the shopping. 'Now, have a nice sleep, you two,' she said. 'Great,' thought Tilly and Tommy. Now they could really have some fun.

In the morning they played hide-and-seek behind the plant pots in the kitchen. 'CRASH!' went the green plant pot all over the floor. Next they played with a ball of wool from the sewing tin. 'CRASH!' went the tin, and everything fell out over the floor.

In the afternoon they played 'Chase the fly around the bedroom'. 'CRASH!' went the china doll, all over the floor. Then they played 'Hunt the spider'. But the spider didn't want to play and ran up and hid in a vase of flowers. 'CRASH!' went the vase, and the water and flowers spilled out across the room.

End
Tommy and Tilly were now very tired. They curled up next to each other and soon fell asleep. A little while later the front door opened. It was their owner returning from shopping.

'Oh dear! What a mess!' she cried. 'I can't have locked the door when I went out. That big, clumsy dog from next door must have got in again.' She smiled fondly at the two little kittens who were still asleep. She had brought them a special treat to eat for tea.

Well, kittens who are always as good as gold deserve a special treat, don't they?

Re-read the story and answer the following questions.

1 What are the two kittens called?

2 What sort of information is given at the beginning of the story?

3 Write these sentences out in your notebook in the correct order.
Tommy and Tilly were now very tired.
'CRASH!' went the china doll, all over the floor.
'Great,' thought Tilly and Tommy.
They lived with their owner in a large house.

4 Which word tells you the sound things made when they fell on the floor?

5 Why did the owner think the dog had got in to her house?

6 What sort of things do you think fell out of the sewing tin?

7 How did the kittens feel after they had finished playing?

8 What sort of special treat do you think the owner had brought back for the kittens?

9 How do you think the owner felt when she opened the door?

10 Pick two lines from the story which tell you that the owner is a lady.

More things to do

Write a story about two pet hamsters that escape from their cage into the garden. You will need to think of a title. In the beginning, say what the hamsters look like. In the middle, say what happens to them. What do they get up to? In the end, write about how they felt.

Explanation

Why is the Sun important?

An **explanation** can tell you why something is important.

Before you read

❋ How does the Sun help us to live?
❋ What would happen if there was no Sun?

Read this explanation.

WHY IS THE SUN IMPORTANT?

The Sun is a huge, hot, bright star. It is important because without it there would be no life on Earth. The Sun gives us light and heat.

All living things need light and heat from the Sun to live. Plants need light and heat to grow. They use the light from the Sun to make food. We cannot make our own food, but plants can. All the food we eat comes from plants in a food chain which starts with the Sun. For instance:

Sun ⟶ potatoes ⟶ chips
Sun ⟶ corn ⟶ hens ⟶ eggs
Sun ⟶ wheat ⟶ bread

Animals need sunlight too. Just like us, their food comes from a food chain which begins with the Sun and the plants.

Sun ⟶ leaf ⟶ caterpillar ⟶ bird
Sun ⟶ seaweed ⟶ small fish ⟶ whale

Sunlight means we can see during the day. If there was no Sun, it would be dark all the time. Even when the sky is cloudy, the sunlight is so strong that it shines through the clouds.

Re-read the explanation and answer the following questions.

1. Which words tell us what the Sun is like?

2. What are the two main things the Sun gives us?

3. Sunlight gives us natural light. Can you think of other things that can give us light?

4. Why can we still see during the day when the sky is cloudy?

5. In your notebook write out these sentences and fill in the missing words.
   All living things need light and heat from the Sun to _____.
   All the food we eat comes from a food _____ which starts with the _____.
   Sunlight means we can see during the _____ even when the sky is cloudy.

6. Why do you think we cannot see the Sun at night-time?

7. In what way do you think the Sun can be harmful?

8. What do you think would happen if there was no Sun? Why?

More things to do

Think of your favourite food. Draw a food chain to show where your food comes from. Underneath your drawing, say what is happening. Remember that your food chain will start with the Sun.

Argument

You should look after your teeth

An **argument** tells you someone's **point of view**.

Before you read
- What does a dentist do?
- Why do you need to clean your teeth?

Read this argument.

YOU SHOULD LOOK AFTER YOUR TEETH

In your lifetime you will have two sets of teeth. The first set of teeth is called milk teeth. When these fall out, adult teeth will grow. Adult teeth will have to last you for the rest of your life.

You should clean your teeth in the morning and before you go to bed. You should also visit your dentist regularly. Eating too many sweets can be bad for your teeth. Chocolate, biscuits and fizzy drinks can have a lot of sugar in them. This sugar can rot your teeth. If your teeth rot, the dentist may have to take them out.

You will only ever have two sets of teeth in your lifetime, so you should look after them carefully.

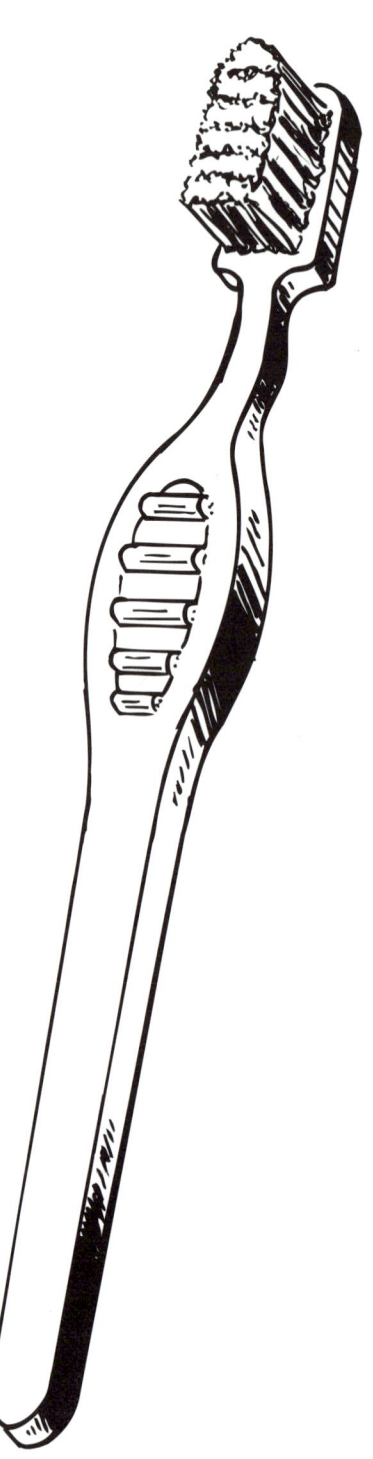

Re-read the argument and answer the following questions.

1 Write this sentence in your notebook and then complete it.
   This argument tells you to ___ ___ ___ ___.

2 How many sets of teeth will you have in your lifetime?

3 What is the first set of teeth called?

4 When will adult teeth grow?

5 How often should you clean your teeth?

6 Which foods are bad for your teeth?

7 What do sweet foods have in them that makes your teeth rot?

8 Why should you go to the dentist?

9 Name two things you can do to look after your teeth.

10 Name some other foods which have a lot of sugar in them.

More things to do

Design a poster which tells people to look after their teeth.
Write down all the food you eat in one day. Which foods do you think have a lot of sugar in them?

Poetry

Unit 17

In our playground

A **poem** sometimes has a beat like music. This is called **rhythm**.

Before you read

❋ Do you enjoy playtime?
❋ Which games do you play in the playground?

Read this poem.

IN OUR PLAYGROUND

In our playground we can run,
And laugh and joke and have some fun,

Children skipping, shouting names,
All of them play different games,

Twirling, pointing, never still,
Lots of things to do until…

The whistle blows, the bell goes…
SILENCE!

Claire Colling

Re-read the poem and answer the following questions.

1 Where are the children playing?

2 Name two things the children are doing in the playground.

3 Pick out two words which tell you how the children are moving in the playground.

4 Do you think the children are happy? Why?

5 What sort of games do you think the children are playing in the poem?

6 What stops the children's fun?

7 How is the playground different at the end of the poem?

8 Say the first line out loud. You can hear the rhythm when you say the poem.
In our playground we can run,
This line has four beats. How many beats does the next line have?

9 Here is another verse about children in the playground. How many beats does each line have?
The children run about
Some laugh, some scream, some shout.

More things to do

Make up your own poem about what happens in the playground.
You can use these rhyming words to help you:

    bell, yell, shout, out   walk, talk, ball, tall
    crunch, lunch, sun, fun   twirl, girl, boy, toy

Does your poem have a rhythm? See if you can count the beats for each line. Read your poem to someone else. Can they work out the rhythm?

Sally Ann – Princess of the Chip Kingdom

This story or **narrative** is about a spoilt, bossy girl called Sally Ann. This story is a **fantasy**. It couldn't really happen.

Before you read

* Make a list of your favourite foods.
* Which foods do you not like?

Read this story.

SALLY ANN – PRINCESS OF THE CHIP KINGDOM

Sally Ann didn't care that no-one liked her. She was selfish, rude, and always wanted her own way. The only thing Sally Ann cared about was eating chips.

On Monday Sally Ann ate chips. On Tuesday Sally Ann ate some more chips. On Wednesday Sally Ann ate lots more chips. On Thursday Sally Ann ate lots and lots of chips. On Friday Sally Ann ate lots and lots and lots of chips. On Saturday Sally Ann ate lots and lots and lots and lots of chips.

'It's not good to eat chips all the time,' everyone used to say.

'I don't like anything else,' screamed Sally Ann. 'I only want chips. Give me chips now!'

One Tuesday in May, Sally Ann was eating some more chips when suddenly one of the chips moved and spoke.

'I am Mr Chipit,' said the chip. 'I can make you Princess of the Chip Kingdom. Close your eyes. Chip-cher-oo.' (That was the magic word.)

When Sally Ann opened her eyes she found herself in Chip Kingdom. There were potatoes everywhere – large ones, small ones, brown ones, red ones, even blue ones!

Sally Ann sat on a throne made from potatoes, eating lots of chips and being rude to everyone. But then Sally Ann got bored. She wanted to go home.

'Chip-cher-oo,' she said and found herself back in the classroom. She opened her mouth to tell the other children what had happened but... out came a potato... and another... and then another.

Sally Ann ran home as fast as she could. On the table her favourite meal was ready. Sally Ann stared at her plate, shaking her head.

Mr Chipit smiled. Sally Ann had learnt her lesson. Do you think she ate any more chips?

Re-read the story and answer the following questions.

1 What kind of girl was Sally Ann?

2 Who told Sally Ann she could be Princess of the Chip Kingdom?

3 What kind of potatoes were there in the Chip Kingdom?

4 What are chips made of?

5 Why do you think Sally got bored?

6 Do you think Sally Ann was eating a healthy diet? Why?

7 Do you think Sally Ann carried on eating chips? Give reasons for your answer.

8 In the story there are days of the week and names of people. These are called proper nouns. All proper nouns begin with a capital letter. Write down all the proper nouns you can find in the story.

More things to do

Write about one of your favourite foods. Think about what it smells like, what it tastes like, what it looks like, where it comes from and why you like it.

How to make cheese on toast

Before you read

- Have you ever helped to make cheese on toast before?
- What is a recipe?

Read these instructions.

HOW TO MAKE CHEESE ON TOAST

This is the list of things you need to make cheese on toast. These are called ingredients.

INGREDIENTS
bread
butter
cheese
sauce or pickle

Here is another list. These are the things you will need to help you make cheese on toast.

cheese grater
knife
grill

INSTRUCTIONS
1. Put the bread under a hot grill.
2. Toast both sides of the bread.
3. Butter one side of the toast.
4. Sprinkle grated cheese on top of the toast.
5. Put the toast back under the grill until the cheese has melted.
6. Spread some sauce or pickle over the top of the melted cheese.

Re-read the recipe and answer the following questions.

1 Write this sentence in your notebook and then complete it.
   This recipe tells you how to make _____ _____ _____.

2 What would you use the knife for?

3 What might you spread on the toast if you didn't have any butter?

4 Why do you think there is a number before each instruction?

5 These instructions are mixed up. Write them in your notebook in the correct order.
   Spread some sauce or pickle over the top of the melted cheese.
   Sprinkle grated cheese on top of the toast.
   Butter one side of the toast.

6 What sort of sauce or pickle might you spread over the cheese on toast?

7 Why does the cheese melt under the grill?

8 What other things can you eat on toast?

9 How else can you toast bread?

More things to do

Write out a recipe for beans on toast, or for one of your own recipes. Remember to list the ingredients. List the things you need to help you make beans on toast. Number the instructions.

Unit 20

Why do some animals sleep in winter?

An **explanation** can tell you why things happen.

Before you read

- What is the weather like in winter?
- Look up the word 'hibernation' in your dictionary. Write down what it means.

Read this explanation.

WHY DO SOME ANIMALS SLEEP IN WINTER?

Some animals sleep in wintertime because the weather can be very cold and it is difficult for them to find food. They can sleep for a long time (from autumn to spring). This kind of winter sleep is called 'hibernation'.

If an animal moves about a lot, it needs food. Animals that hibernate do not need to eat much because they are not moving about. Their hearts beat very slowly and they also breathe slowly. They find a place that is sheltered from bad weather and where they are out of danger. Their body fat keeps them alive and warm.

Some animals which hibernate in wintertime are dormice, hedgehogs, chipmunks, bears and frogs.

Some animals, such as the hedgehog, may wake up from their hibernation and then go back to sleep again. The hedgehog may wake up every two to three days, feed on a worm and then go back to sleep.

When the weather becomes warmer in spring, the animals start to wake up and look for food.

Re-read the explanation and answer the following questions.

1 Why do some animals hibernate in winter?

2 What happens to an animal's body when it hibernates?

3 When animals hibernate, they need to find a place where they are 'out of danger'. Why do you think they need to do this?

4 Name three animals which hibernate.

5 Why might an animal wake up during hibernation?

6 When do animals stop hibernating?

7 Where do you think hedgehogs might find a sheltered place to hibernate?

8 Why is it harder for animals to find food in winter?

9 In your notebooks copy out the sentences below about frogs. Fill in the spaces using these words: place, feed, pond, mud

When frogs hibernate they swim to the bottom of a _____ and cover themselves in _____ .
Frogs do not _____ at all during the winter.
There are sometimes many frogs together in the same _____ .

More things to do

Write your own explanation which tells people why bats hibernate. Use these words to help you:

dark	cave	upside-down	cold weather
hibernate	breathe slowly	heart beats slowly	sleep in groups
body fat keeps them alive		bodies are cold	food is scarce

Explanation

Being able to swim can save your life

An **argument** gives a view about something and **reasons** for that **point of view**.

Before you read

- How well can you swim?
- Why is it important to learn how to swim?

Read this argument.

BEING ABLE TO SWIM CAN SAVE YOUR LIFE

It is important to learn how to swim because one day it could save your life. If you could not swim and you fell into deep water you could drown.

You can find deep water in many places. You may live close to a lake or canal. If you fell in you would need to be able to swim to the side and climb out.

When you have swimming lessons in school, you can learn how to swim different strokes, such as the front crawl, breaststroke and backstroke. These will help you become a strong swimmer.

There are many swimming baths where you can learn how to swim, and there are pool rules which tell you how to behave safely in the water and on the side of the pool.

Swimming is also fun and good for you. You can enjoy going swimming with your family and friends. It is also good exercise and helps to keep you fit.

But the main argument for being able to swim is that, one day, it could save your life.

Re-read the argument and answer the following questions.

1 What is the main point of the argument?

2 If you could not swim and you fell into deep water, what could happen to you?

3 Canals and lakes are examples of deep water. Can you think of some other examples?

4 Why is swimming good exercise?

5 Can you think of two safety rules that you might find at the swimming baths?

6 As well as swimming different strokes, what other things can you do in the water?

7 Why do you think it is important to practise climbing out of the pool without using the steps?

8 Arguments use words such as: because, if, so, unless. Write these sentences in your notebook and fill in the spaces using these words.
if, so, unless, because

Swimming is good for you _____ it keeps you fit.
You should not go near deep water _____ you can swim.
You learn different swimming strokes _____ that you may become a strong swimmer.
You can drown in deep water _____ you do not know how to swim.

9 Which swimming strokes might you learn in school?

More things to do

Write an argument in which the main idea is that safety rules are important at the swimming baths. Here are some words to help you:

running   dangerous   slippery   hurt   pushing
diving   shallow   eating   ducking   deep end
non-swimmers

Argument

Unit 22

Exercise is good for you!

An **argument** tells you someone's **point of view**. It **sums up** their view at the end.

Before you read

❂ Look up the word 'exercise' in your dictionary. What does it mean?
❂ Why do you need to exercise?

Read this argument.

EXERCISE IS GOOD FOR YOU!

Exercise is good for you because it can help you to keep fit and healthy. It is not enough just to eat a healthy diet. Exercise is important too. Exercise will make your muscles stronger. There are about 600 muscles in the body. They move your bones and let you move your joints. If you do not exercise your muscles, they will be weaker and smaller.

One of the most important muscles in the body is the heart. To exercise your heart, you need to do something like swimming, or playing a game in which you run about. This will make you breathe more deeply and make your heart and lungs stronger.

One of the places where you can exercise is at school. In school, children have PE lessons which help them to keep fit and well. Try to exercise at least three times a week because exercise is good for you!

Re-read the argument and answer the following questions.

1 Write these sentences in your notebook and then complete them.
   Exercise will make your muscles _____.
   There are about _____ muscles in the body.
   One of the most important muscles in the body is the _____.

2 What is the main idea in this argument?

3 Where are the muscles which help you to move about?

4 What will happen to your muscles if you do not exercise?

5 Which exercises does the writer say are good for the heart? (Think of games where you run about.)

6 What sort of exercise do you do in school?

7 Where would you find a joint in the body?

8 How does the author 'sum up' the argument. (Look at the final sentence.)

9 Where else can you exercise, apart from school?

10 Find your pulse. (Your pulse tells you how fast your heart is beating.) Write down what you think happens to your pulse when you exercise. Try it out!

More things to do

Write a short argument which tells people to eat more fruit. Remember to say why fruit is good for people to eat.

Poetry

Unit 23

Time flies

Poems sometimes have a special message.

Before you read

❊ What do you do in your spare time?
❊ Why can time be precious?

Read this poem about time.

TIME FLIES

Time is passing, tick tock tick,
Don't idle away! Come on, be quick!
Time is passing, tock tick tock,
See the hands move round the clock.

Sometimes it seems that time stands still,
When we are bored, or sad, or ill...
We want the empty hours to end,
But time forgets to be our friend.

Yet when there's something we enjoy,
A game, a dance, a favourite toy,
To hold the moments back we try,
But time says 'Sorry, I must fly!'

Seconds, minutes, hours and days,
Are ours to fill in many ways,
So wisely choose the things you do,
For time won't wait for me or you!

Claire Colling

Re-read the poem and answer the following questions.

1 What is the poem about?

2 Which hands would you find on a clock?

3 What else can we use to tell the time?

4 Which words in the poem describe the sound the clock is making?

5 When does time seem to stand still?

6 Read the last verse. What do you think the special message is in this poem?

7 Write down the line which tells you not to be lazy.

8 Think of a different title you could call this poem.

9 In what way do you think you make good use of your time?

More things to do

Finish off this verse of the poem in your notebooks. Put these words in the right places:

time   happy   clock   run

But when we're _____ having fun,
That's when _____ begins to _____ .
Time is passing, tock tick tock,
See the hands move round the _____ .

Now work out the rhythm of the poem. How many beats are there on each line?

The strange plant

In this story there are many **adjectives**. Adjectives **describe** things.

Before you read

- Can you name any parts of a plant?
- Describe a plant which grows in your garden, in your house, or in the classroom.

Read this story.

THE STRANGE PLANT

Jake had lost the ball at the bottom of the garden. He was trying to find it. 'Come and look at this!' shouted Jake, suddenly. He saw a very strange-looking plant growing among the weeds.

'Wow!' said Samantha. She had looked at many different plants in school before, but she had never seen anything like this.

The tall, weird plant had a long blue stalk. At the top of the stalk there was a golden flower which had red petals with yellow spots. The leaves were thin, long and spiky, and the plant gave off a sweet smell.

Jake put out his hand to touch the plant. All of a sudden it made a strange sound and started shaking. Its leaves started moving upwards as if it were stretching. One of its roots tore itself out of the ground, then another and another.

Jake and Samantha wanted to run because they were scared, but they couldn't help but watch to see what would happen next...

Re-read the story and answer the following questions.

1 Where were Samantha and Jake playing when they found the plant?

2 Pick out three adjectives (describing words) which describe the plant.

3 Why did Jake and Samantha not run away?

4 Why did Samantha think it was a strange plant?

5 Pick out another word in the story which means the same as 'strange'.

6 How do you think Samantha and Jake felt when they first found the plant?

7 What happened when Jake tried to touch the plant?

8 What do you think happened next in the story?

9 What do you think would be a good ending for the story?

More things to do

Imagine you find a strange plant in your garden. What do the roots, petals, leaves, stalks and flowers look like? How does it move? Is it friendly or unfriendly? Where does it come from? What does it eat? Describe your plant in a lot of detail, then ask someone else to draw your plant from your description.

Unit 25

Narrative

The magic pencil

A **narrative** tells a story. In this narrative the main character Mark has quite a shock in his art lesson!

Before you read

* Do you enjoy art lessons?
* Look at the title. Can you guess what the story is about?

Read this story.

THE MAGIC PENCIL

At one o'clock the teacher handed out new green pencils to the class for the art lesson.

'Hey ginger long legs,' said one unkind girl to Mark. 'What are you going to draw?'

Mark flicked the red hair from his face and didn't know what to say. He sat at his desk. He could feel his big blue eyes filling up with tears.

'What can I do?' he asked his friend Matthew. 'I don't know what to draw. I'm no good at drawing.'

Well, I'm going to draw my bike,' said Matthew. 'Have you got a bike or maybe a pet you can draw?'

Mark thought long and hard, but he couldn't think of anything to draw. Then a strange thing happened. As Mark picked up the pencil, it began to shake and twitch. Mark held on to the pencil tightly. Then it began to draw a picture on the blank piece of paper. It was wonderful!

At the end of the lesson, everyone admired Mark's work.

'How ever did you draw that?' they asked. 'It's great!' Mark had a smile on his face for the rest of the day. When it was time to go home, Mark looked for the pencil on his desk but it had gone.

He wondered where it might end up next!

Re-read the story and answer the following questions.

1 Where does the story take place?

2 Pick out two sentences from the story that tell you what Mark looks like?

3 Why was Mark sad?

4 Which two words tell you how the magic pencil moved.

5 Why was the pencil a magic one?

6 How do you think Mark felt when the pencil started to move?

7 What do you think the magic pencil drew?

8 Where do you think the pencil is now?

9 Do you think Mark would have told his friends about the magic pencil? Why?

10 In the story, question marks are used when questions are asked. For example, 'What can I do?'
   a Write down two other sentences from this story where question marks are used.
   b Write down a question you would like to ask Mark about the pencil.

More things to do

Draw the picture you think the magic pencil drew.
Imagine that you find a magic maths pencil. Write a story about what happens in class.

Unit 26

On the beach

This is a **poem** about enjoying the seaside. Poems are sometimes split into **verses** like the one you are going to read.

Before you read

- Think of some words which describe the weather.
- What has the weather been like today?

Read this poem.

ON THE BEACH

In howling wind and heavy rain,
The waves are crashing again and again,
Hear the ROAR the sea is making
With every giant breath it's taking.
In the dark sky the seagulls screech,
And no-one plays upon the beach.

But when the bright sun shows its face,
The beach is now a different place,
Sandcastles, deckchairs, ice-creams too,
With buckets and spades there's lots to do.
Children laughing, hand in hand,
They skip and run along the sand.

But now the sun must go to bed,
And rest its bright and weary head,
The children now must leave the shore,
Then sand and sea are quiet once more,
The sunset marks the end of day,
And castles now are swept away.

Claire Colling

Re-read the poem and answer the following questions.

1. What type of noise does the poet say the sea makes?

2. Think of another word which could describe the noise of the sea.

3. In the first verse, do you think the weather is good or bad? Why?

4. In which type of weather would you like to be on the beach? Why?

5. In the third verse, why do you think the children have gone home?

6. In the first verse, what do you think the poet means when she says that the sea is 'taking a breath'?

7. Why do you think the poet has written the word ROAR in capitals in the first verse?

8. Which seasons of the year do you think the poet is writing about? Why?

9. In the final verse, where do you think all the sandcastles have gone?

10. Words which have the same sounds at the ends are called rhymes. Poems can rhyme like this one – but they don't have to. In your notebook, write down three pairs of rhyming words. For example, hand, sand.

More things to do

Using your weather words, write one verse of a poem which describes the weather. Remember, it doesn't have to rhyme!

Unit 27

Drama

In the rainforest

When you listen to a radio play, you cannot see what is taking place. **Sound effects** are needed so that people can imagine what is happening.

Before you read

- What might you find in a rainforest?
- What are some of the sounds you might hear in a rainforest?

Here are the characters in the play: Hanif Megan

Read this play.

IN THE RAINFOREST

In the distance can be heard the sound of wood being chopped. Leaves are rustling gently in the breeze.

HANIF: Have you ever been to a rainforest before, Megan?
(Sound of twigs breaking under their feet, leaves rustling.)
MEGAN: *(in a shaking voice)* No, I haven't, but I've heard about all the scary things you can find in a rainforest, like tigers and...
(A parrot squawks.) What was that?
HANIF: Don't worry, it's only a parrot, it won't hurt you.
MEGAN: Yes, but what about all the spiders and other creepy crawlies you can find here?
HANIF: What, like that snake, you mean?
(Sound of hissing snake.)
MEGAN: *(shouting)* Help!
HANIF: Be quiet, you'll scare it away. It won't hurt you – that one's not poisonous.
MEGAN: I wish I hadn't come here.
HANIF: *(whispering)* Sssh! Listen!
MEGAN: *(whispering)* What is it?
(Sound of water dripping on to leaf.)
HANIF: I think it's starting to rain. Can you hear that hummingbird too? *(Hummingbird flutters its wings.)*
MEGAN: Look up there. In those enormous trees!
(Monkey makes a sound as it swings through the branches. More

rustling of leaves and snapping of twigs as Hanif and Megan carry on walking.)
HANIF: Look! Over here! Look at that amazing tiger. It's drinking from that puddle.
(Tiger laps up water.)
MEGAN: Yes it is wonderful but let's not get too close.
HANIF: Let's sit down here by the waterfall for a moment.
MEGAN: Hanif, I've changed my mind about the rainforest. It's a lovely place, not scary at all. There are so many beautiful animals and plants here.
HANIF: Yes, I just wish everyone would think like that and stop chopping the trees down.
(Sound of wood being chopped.)

Re-read the play and answer the following questions.

1 Where are Hanif and Megan?

2 Which animal makes a squawking sound?

3 Why does Megan speak with a shaking voice to begin with?

4 Pick a line which tells you that Hanif is not afraid of the animals.

5 Name three animals Hanif and Megan see in the rainforest.

6 Why are the sound effects important in this play?

7 How would chopping down the rainforest affect the animals?

8 Do you know why people chop rainforests down?

9 List the sound effects you need in this play.

More things to do

Act out the play. You will need two characters and people to help with

Unit 28

A trip to the future

A **narrative** tells a story and has one or more characters.

Before you read

- Would you like to travel into the future?
- Who would you take with you?

Read this story.

A TRIP TO THE FUTURE

Leon and Surinder were looking at the toy cars at the back of the toyshop. As Leon turned round, he saw a dusty sheet covering something in the corner of the room. A big sign on the front said 'Do Not Touch!'

Leon, who never took any notice of signs like that, reached out his hand and...

'Do not touch!' cried Surinder. 'It says 'Do not touch!'' As she spoke, a strange green light started glowing under the sheet.

Both children peered under the sheet to see what was there. It was an old rusty motorbike. It had a computer keyboard at the front and there were lots of buttons and flashing lights.

'This is great!' said Surinder. 'It's like one of those video games!'

They both got on the bike. Leon sat at the front pressing the buttons, and Surinder sat behind him. Leon pressed the red button and tried to get a picture on the computer screen.

All of a sudden the bike started to move. It began shaking and whizzing around.

Stop!' shouted Surinder. 'I want to get off!'

But it was too late. Leon had pressed the button on the time machine marked 'FUTURE'...

Re-read the story and answer the following questions.

1 Who are the characters in the story?

2 Where were the children looking at toy cars?

3 What did the big sign say?

4 What colour light was glowing under the sheet?

5 What did the children find under the sheet?

6 What do you think the buttons were for on the bike?

7 Why did Surinder want to get off the bike?

8 What are two important things that have happened so far in this story?

9 How do you think the children felt about going into the future?

10 Exclamation marks are used to make something stand out. For example, Do not touch! Stop! Pick out two other sentences where exclamation marks have been used.

More things to do

Write about what Leon and Surinder might see in the future.
Think about where the motorbike will take the children, what Leon and Surinder will see there, how things will be different in the future, what the houses and cars will look like, what people will be wearing.

Unit 29

How a guitar makes a sound

An **explanation** can tell you how things work.

Before you read

- Do you know the names of any musical instruments?
- Have you ever played a musical instrument?

Read this explanation.

HOW A GUITAR MAKES A SOUND

A guitar is a musical instrument with strings. There are six strings on the guitar made of steel or nylon. An ordinary guitar is empty inside.

To make a sound on the guitar, you can pluck the strings with your fingers. When you pluck a guitar string it shakes or vibrates. The string that vibrates makes the air all around it move about. It is the air moving about that causes the sound. The sound hole makes the sound louder.

You can change the sounds the guitar makes by making the strings longer or shorter. You can make the strings longer or shorter by moving the pegs at the top of the guitar, or by pressing your fingers on the string. A long string will make a low sound. A short string will make a high sound.

Electric guitars do not have a sound hole. They are stronger than ordinary guitars because they use electricity to make the sounds louder.

Re-read the explanation and answer the following questions.

1. What are the strings on a guitar made of?

2. Name any other instruments that have strings.

3. How can you make a sound on the guitar?

4. Pick out a word that tells you how the string moves when it is plucked?

5. How can you change the sound a guitar makes?

6. How is an electric guitar different to an ordinary guitar?

7. Do you think a piano has strings? Why?

8. You use your fingers to pluck the strings on a guitar. What do you use to play a violin?

9. In this explanation, there are some difficult words. Can you explain what they mean? (You might need to use a dictionary.)
   pluck
   vibrate

More things to do

You can play instruments in different ways to make sounds. Can you think of any instruments you would play like this?
   blow   pluck   shake   tap

Here are the names of some instruments to help you.
   tambourine   recorder   harp   triangle

Unit 30

Report

Dinosaurs

A **report** contains **facts**. A fact tells you about something which is true.

Before you read

❖ What is a reptile?
❖ How do you know what dinosaurs looked like?

Read this report.

DINOSAURS

Dinosaurs were reptiles. They had scaly skin and lived on earth millions of years ago. Dinosaurs are the largest animals ever to have lived on earth.

People know about dinosaurs because dinosaur bones have been found in the ground. These old dinosaur bones are called fossils. Bones can be examined and put together to find out what sort of dinosaur it is. It's a bit like doing a giant jigsaw puzzle!

There were lots of different dinosaurs, both small and large. Some dinosaurs ate meat, some ate only plants.

Tyrannosaurus Rex (T-Rex) was the biggest meat eater. Its teeth were huge. It could run after its prey with its strong back legs. It could run at 50 kilometres per hour. It was 14 metres long and five metres tall.

Stegosaurus was a plant eater. It had an enormous body, but only a small head. There were large spikes on its tail and it could swish it from side to side.

Triceratops had an enormous head with three sharp horns. It had a frill around its neck with spikes on. Triceratops was a plant eater.

One of the largest dinosaurs was Diplodocus. It was 27 metres long and was a plant eater. Diplodocus had a very long neck and tail.

People think that dinosaurs were wiped out when a huge rock, called a meteor, hit Earth. Only very small animals, such as insects and tiny reptiles, survived.

Re-read the report and answer the following questions.

1. How do we know that dinosaurs lived millions of years ago?

2. Which dinosaur does the report tell us about first?

3. Why do you think Diplodocus had a very long neck?

4. Can you think of an animal which is alive now that has a very long neck?

5. Which dinosaur had horns?

6. In your notebooks, fill in the missing words.
   Old dinosaur bones are called _____.
   Stegosaurus was a _____ eater.
   They had scaly skin and lived on earth _____ of years ago.

7. Huge is one adjective (describing word) which describes how big some of the dinosaurs were. Write down two other adjectives which mean the same thing.

8. How did T-Rex get its food?

9. Imagine what it would have been like if people were alive at the same time as dinosaurs. Would you have liked to have lived when they were on earth? Why?

More things to do

Write a short report describing what you think it was like when the meteor hit earth. Use the phrases below to help you:

meteor   skies   dust   noisy   windy
darkness for months   animals running and flying
64 million years ago